VISUAL THEOLOGY

STUDY GUIDE

VISUAL THEOLOGY

SEEING AND UNDERSTANDING
THE TRUTH ABOUT GOD

STUDY GUIDE

TIM CHALLIES AND JOSH BYERS
WITH ZACH DIETRICH

ZONDERVAN

Visual Theology Study Guide
Copyright © 2018 by Tim Challies and Josh Byers

This title is also available as a Zondervan ebook.

Requests for information should be addressed to:
Zondervan, *3900 Sparks Dr. SE, Grand Rapids, Michigan 49546*

ISBN 978-0-310-57625-9

Published in association with the literary agency of Wolgemuth & Associates, Inc.

Cover design: Studio Gearbox
Interior illustrations: Josh Byers
Interior design: Josh Byers and Kait Lamphere

Printed in the United States of America

22 23 24 25 26 27 /LSC/ 20 19 18 17 16 15 14 13 12 11 10 9 8 7 6 5 4

CONTENTS

HOW TO USE THIS STUDY GUIDE

This study guide is designed to help you grow in godliness by practicing what you learn in *Visual Theology*. Since growth in godliness is both personal and communal, the study guide has both personal and small group studies. Here's what you'll find for each chapter:

BIG PICTURE

These are the main themes you'll focus on in the group study.

KEY TERMS

This section is an opportunity to grow your vocabulary by gathering your own definitions. There are additional Scriptures to read for each term.

GROUP STUDY

Your group studies will be most effective if participants read both the book chapter and the study before you meet. It should take you about 45 minutes to an hour to complete your study. Each study is divided into three divisions:

REFLECT

Start by reflecting on a specific situation or story from your life that relates to the chapter. What you do and what you think are windows into your heart. Don't worry about being critical or fixing things yet. Just tell your stories and then reflect on them.

ENCOUNTER

God's Word speaks into every area of your life. Now look in the Bible to see what God says about the gospel and growth. As with the book, we've included visual elements in order to grow your understanding and to make it more fun!

TRANSFORM

The goal of the study is personal growth in godliness. In light of God's Word, both in the chapter and the study guide, talk about what needs to be different and how it will happen.

PERSONAL REFLECTION

This section helps you think reflectively about what you have learned in each chapter. You can work through this section on your own before or after your group study.

The reflection section is drawn from the book of Colossians, and it contains Scripture readings and personal assignments to practice the truths you are learning. Colossians is about growth in the gospel. The apostle Paul was worried that the church would be tempted away from Christ and the gospel, and his letter teaches us how the gospel is sufficient for us to know Christ and become like him.

Chapter 1	Gospel	Read Colossians
Chapter 2	Identity	Colossians 1:1–8
Chapter 3	Relationship	Colossians 1:9–14
Chapter 4	Drama	Colossians 1:15–23
Chapter 5	Doctrine	Colossians 2:1–23
Chapter 6	Putting Off	Colossians 3:1–11
Chapter 7	Putting On	Colossians 3:12–17
Chapter 8	Vocation	Colossians 3:22–4:1
Chapter 9	Relationships	Colossians 3:18–4:1
Chapter 10	Stewardship	Colossians 4:5–18

VISUALIZE

If you're an artist or visual learner, you know that the creative process is a chance to learn through visualizing. Regardless of your artistic ability, this section invites you to "illustrate" theology in pictures or words so that its truths might root more deeply in your life. We'd love to see your work, so share with us on Twitter using the hashtag #visualtheology or our Facebook page: facebook.com/visualtheology.

> "I pray that the eyes of your heart may be enlightened in order that you may know the hope to which he has called you, the riches of his glorious inheritance in his holy people, and his incomparably great power for us who believe."
>
> *(Ephesians 1:18–19 NIV)*

LEADING A GROUP STUDY

Make your discussion more engaging by utilizing visuals. You can refer to posters or the book illustrations, or use presentation software, a whiteboard, or even a large piece of paper for notes and diagrams—whatever you think might help participants grow in their understanding. PowerPoint slides to supplement teaching or group discussion as well as additional posters and downloads are available at the *Visual Theology* website—visualtheology.church.

Prepare prior to each session by reading the selected chapters in *Visual Theology* and completing the group study. This will help you anticipate questions and gather any additional supplies you may need.

Clearly communicate to participants what is expected from them regarding the reading and homework assignments. Make sure everyone understands where and when you are meeting.

Model good discussion for your group. Be willing to share your own stories and struggles without dominating the conversation. If you're willing to be open, you'll encourage them to do the same.

Don't interrupt when someone is sharing during the meeting. Encourage participants by acknowledging them and thanking them when they speak up. Do the hard work of being quiet and waiting until they are finished sharing.

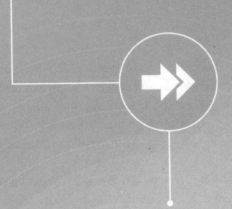

CHAPTER ONE
GOSPEL

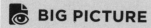 BIG PICTURE

"The moment I stop repeating it is the moment I begin forgetting it." (Visual Theology, 17)

- Learn how to recount the gospel every day—to yourself and with others.
- We never move beyond our need for the gospel and its transforming power.

KEY TERMS TO DEFINE

- **Gospel** (*VT*, 18; 1 Corinthians 15:1–4)
- **Preach** (*VT*, 21; Romans 1:8–16; 1 Timothy 1:12–17)
- **Evangelize** (*VT*, 24; Matthew 18:18–20; Luke 8:39)
- **Worship** (*VT*, 25; Colossians 3:15–17)
- **Ordinances** (*VT*, 25–27; Matthew 28:18–20; Romans 6:1–4; 1 Corinthians 11:27–33)

GROUP STUDY

REFLECT

1. What do you most commonly forget (e.g., names, dates, etc.)? What do you typically do to help yourself remember something you have forgotten?

2. Tim described four ways of recounting the gospel in chapter one of *Visual Theology*. Describe how God has used one of these ways in your life to grow your love for Christ.

🔲 ENCOUNTER

Some people's encounter with the gospel is so profound that it turns their lives entirely upside down. The addict never uses again. The former atheist believes in God. Jesus so transforms them that they literally become a new person overnight. For others, conversion is special but may feel like just another day of the week. Some Christians even become embarrassed by "how boring their story is." The problem is that we look at our salvation through human eyes. However, if we are to remain rooted in the gospel, we need to look at our lives with an eternal perspective that fully grasps the depths of our problem and the greatness of the gospel. This is Paul's perspective in Ephesians 2:1–10. He begins by painting an unflattering picture of us without Christ but ends by calling us God's work of art. Read and study about our amazing gospel transformation in these verses.

> [1] And you were dead in the trespasses and sins [2] in which you once walked, following the course of this world, following the prince of the power of the air, the spirit that is now at work in the sons of disobedience— [3] among whom we all once lived in the passions of our flesh, carrying out the desires of the body and the mind, and were by nature children of wrath, like the rest of mankind. [4] But God, being rich in mercy, because of the great love with which he loved us, [5] even when we were dead in our trespasses, made us alive together with Christ—by grace you have been saved— [6] and raised us up with him and seated us with him in the heavenly places in Christ Jesus, [7] so that in the coming ages he might show the immeasurable riches of his grace in kindness toward us in Christ Jesus. [8] For by grace you have been saved through faith. And this is not your own doing; it is the gift of God, [9] not a result of works, so that no one may boast. [10] For we are his workmanship, created in Christ Jesus for good works, which God prepared beforehand, that we should walk in them.

3. On the next page complete the infographic, making a list of all the ways we are described without Christ. Draw lines connecting "without Christ" to "with Christ" to show our gospel transformation. For example, we were dead in sins; now we are alive with Christ.

EPHESIANS 2:1-10

WITHOUT CHRIST vs WITH CHRIST

BUT BECAUSE OF HIS GREAT LOVE FOR US GOD WHO IS RICH IN MERCY

4. Read how the apostle Paul recounts the gospel in his own life in 1 Timothy 1:12–17.

> [12] I thank him who has given me strength, Christ Jesus our Lord, because he judged me faithful, appointing me to his service, [13] though formerly I was a blasphemer, persecutor, and insolent opponent. But I received mercy because I had acted ignorantly in unbelief, [14] and the grace of our Lord overflowed for me with the faith and love that are in Christ Jesus. [15] The saying is trustworthy and deserving of full acceptance, that Christ Jesus came into the world to save sinners, of whom I am the foremost. [16] But I received mercy for this reason, that in me, as the foremost, Jesus Christ might display his perfect patience as an example to those who were to believe in him for eternal life. [17] To the King of the ages, immortal, invisible, the only God, be honor and glory forever and ever. Amen.

How does he describe the facts of the gospel? What about his own experience of the gospel?

 TRANSFORM

5. The gospel is both factual and relational. Why are both parts necessary? What are the dangers of having one but not the other in your experience of the gospel?

6. "Many Christians live with the sad delusion that the gospel is only the entranceway to the Christian life. They believe that the gospel gets you in, but then you need to advance to deeds, creeds, and meeting needs. But the good news never becomes old news" (*VT*, 21). What do you think Tim means when he talks about moving "beyond the gospel"? Why is this a mistake?

7. How have you personally experienced God's grace in the gospel? Share one or two examples.

PERSONAL REFLECTION

1. Tim describes the effect of evangelism like this: "Rarely are you given a deeper and clearer sense of Christ's love and presence than when you are declaring all the great things he has done in your heart and in your life" (*VT*, 25). Make a list of all the wonderful things Christ has done for you.

2. What are some practical ways you can share the story of your conversion with someone? How do you communicate the gospel (facts and relationship) through your story?

3. Colossians is about growth in the gospel. The apostle Paul worried that the church might be tempted away from Christ and the gospel. This letter shows how the gospel is sufficient for us to know Christ and become like him. This week, read Colossians from start to finish in either one sitting or over a few days. Pray for God to grow your love of the gospel and Jesus Christ, and then consider the following questions:

Who is the author?

Who are the recipients?

What are the major themes of the letter?

What verses stand out to you after your first reading? Why?

▲ VISUALIZE

"The gospel is not only the gateway into the Christian life, but the pathway of the Christian life."—Dane Ortlund (*VT*, 21)*

Visualize your life without Christ and your life with Christ as described Ephesians 2:1–10. Draw something (artistry not required!), paste photos from a magazine, jot down a meaningful quote, whatever helps you best picture and internalize this scriptural truth.

---

* Dane Ortlund, "What's All This 'Gospel Centered' Talk About?" Boundless.org, July 14, 2014, www.boundless .org/faith/2014/whats-all-this-gospel-centered-talk-about (accessed July 31, 2015).

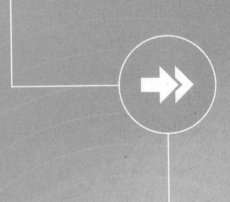

SECTION ONE
GROW CLOSE TO CHRIST

CHAPTER TWO
IDENTITY

BIG PICTURE

"As you attempt to live a spiritually healthy life and as you grow close to Christ, it is absolutely crucial that you understand who you have become and who you are." (*VT*, 29)

- Our foundational new identity is "in Christ."
- "In Christ" overshadows every other identity we have.

KEY TERMS TO DEFINE

- **Justification** (*VT*, 33; Romans 3:20–24; Romans 5:9; Romans 8:1; Galatians 3)
- **Adoption** (*VT*, 34; John 1:12; Romans 8:15–16; Galatians 4:4–5; Ephesians 1:5)
- **Trinity** (*VT*, 34; Matthew 28:19–20; 2 Corinthians 13:14)

GROUP STUDY

REFLECT

1. What is your favorite movie? How many times have you seen it? What makes this movie your favorite?

Each year, Dictionary.com selects a word of the year that they think best captures the big picture of the year. As editors reviewed online searches and news, they observed how many "headlines tied to gender, sexuality and race dominated the news." The editors wrote, "In particular, many of the year's biggest stories focused on the way in which individuals or members of a group are perceived, understood, accepted or shut out." The Word of the Year winner for 2015: Identity.* Our society has become obsessed with personal identity. People find their identity through a countless combination of possessions, occupations, relationships, and experiences.

---

* http://time.com/4139350/dictionary-2015-word-of-the-year/ (accessed May 3, 2016).

2. Make a list of identities common in our society. Think in terms of categories (e.g., occupations/activities, psychological labels, experiences, and backgrounds).

3. What identities tend to shape how you see yourself? If you are working on these questions with a group, discuss any trends or similarities you notice in your group. Are there any differences? If so, what are they?

🗨 ENCOUNTER

4. Every person has a unique story. Every story has countless possibilities. That means there are nearly infinite plotlines possible in this world. The Bible embraces the complexities of our individual identities, and yet the Bible is refreshingly simple when it teaches that we all play one of two different parts. We are either "in Adam" or "in Christ." Study the passages in the infographic on the next page and write down what you learn about being "in Christ" and "in Adam."

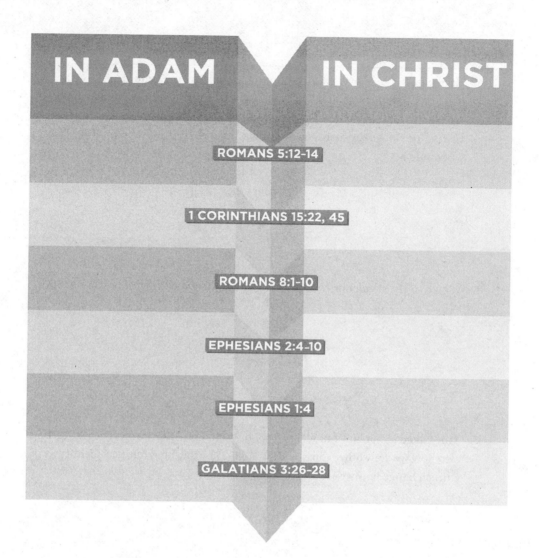

IN ADAM   IN CHRIST

ROMANS 5:12-14

1 CORINTHIANS 15:22, 45

ROMANS 8:1-10

EPHESIANS 2:4-10

EPHESIANS 1:4

GALATIANS 3:26-28

5. Summarize what it means to be "in Adam." What does it mean to be "in Christ"?

6. "It is impossible to overstate the importance of knowing your identity—who you are in relation to Christ" (*VT*, 38). Does the truth that all of us are either "in Christ" or "in Adam" help you or bother you? How does this identity—"in Christ" or "in Adam"—shape how we should live? How we should think? How we should act?

7. Which of the six identities in chapter two are most meaningful to you right now? Why?

8. Tim talked about how our identity not only changes how we view ourselves, but also how we view other Christians (*VT*, 34–37). How does our new identity in Christ change how we see and relate to others?

1. What comes to mind when you think of discipline? In what sense is it a sign of God's love that we receive his discipline?

2. "Being adopted means you can relate to other Christians as brothers, sisters, fathers, and mothers. It assures you that your relationships with other Christians are deep and meaningful" (*VT*, 35). What are some ways in which relationships with other believers are different than relationships with those who do not follow Christ?

3. A reoccurring theme in chapter two of *Visual Theology* is fear. Fear of offending God. Fear of the future. Fear of Satan. What fears typically affect you? How does knowing your identity and God's promises help to counter that fear?

4. Read and think about Colossians 1:1–8.

    [1] Paul, an apostle of Christ Jesus by the will of God, and Timothy our brother,
    [2] To the saints and faithful brothers in Christ at Colossae:
    Grace to you and peace from God our Father.
    [3] We always thank God, the Father of our Lord Jesus Christ, when we pray for you, [4] since we heard of your faith in Christ Jesus and of the love that you

have for all the saints, [5] because of the hope laid up for you in heaven. Of this you have heard before in the word of the truth, the gospel, [6] which has come to you, as indeed in the whole world it is bearing fruit and increasing—as it also does among you, since the day you heard it and understood the grace of God in truth, [7] just as you learned it from Epaphras our beloved fellow servant. He is a faithful minister of Christ on your behalf, [8] and has made known to us your love in the Spirit.

What does Paul thank God for?

How does Paul describe the gospel?

Pray, using Colossians 1:1–8 as a guide for giving thanks to God for the gospel.

VISUALIZE

"I am the vine; you are the branches." (John 15:5)

- "There are past, present, and future dimensions to this union [with Christ]" (*VT*, 30–32).
- "*Justified* is a term that comes from the world of law, from the courtroom" (*VT*, 33).

Use the next page to visualize this "vine and branches" imagery with pictures, photos, or words. Or celebrate your "in Christ" identity with images, perhaps illustrating how that identity has power over your greatest fears.

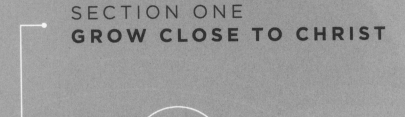

CHAPTER THREE
RELATIONSHIP

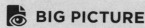 BIG PICTURE

"The more we commit to Bible reading and to prayer, the more of our lives we spend communing with God." (VT, 41)

- We need to grow in our understanding of the power of God's Word and the privilege of prayer.
- Begin to understand the relationship between the Bible and prayer.

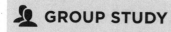 KEY TERMS TO DEFINE

- **Inspiration** (*VT*, 47; 2 Timothy 3:16–17; 2 Peter 1:21)
- **Illumination** (*VT*, 48; Psalm 119:18; 2 Corinthians 2:14–15)

 GROUP STUDY

REFLECT

1. The past twenty years have seen radical shifts in technology and the way we communicate. How has the technological revolution changed the way you communicate? How is it better? How are things worse?

2. Look back at the past two weeks and reflect on your communication with God. If you were describing your relationship with God as one friend to another, what words might you use? What tools help your relationship? What obstacles hinder your relationship?

3. If you had to plot your Bible reading and prayer, what would it look like? (Use the graphic below.) How could this be a helpful or dangerous way to assess your relationship?

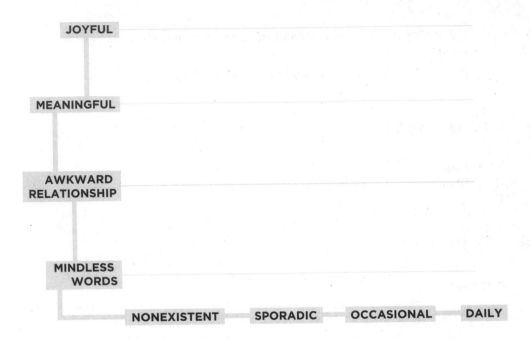

ENCOUNTER

"Christianity offers a genuine relationship with the living God. I don't think I can say it too many times" (*VT*, 59). Our relationship with God begins with the gospel, and it includes many things in addition to the gospel, but it never moves beyond the gospel. Our relationship with God gives us a new identity. We are free from the weight of past guilt, the power of present sin, and the fear of future judgment. The author of Hebrews uses one word to sum up the happiness of our relationship with God: *rest*. We rest from our labors and enjoy God's presence. We long for the day when we will rest in the presence of God in heaven, but even now we can be at rest in our relationship with him. However, because our hearts are deceptive, we must make every effort to rest our relationship on God's promises and not our abilities.

Hebrews 4:12–16 (below) talks about both the power of God's Word and the privilege of prayer. The Word fully exposes who we are before God. Being fully known by God and exposed by his Word (the Law) is terrifying. But because of the Word that God speaks in the gospel, as sinners we can draw near to the throne of grace with confidence.

12 For the word of God is living and active, sharper than any two-edged sword, piercing to the division of soul and of spirit, of joints and of marrow, and discerning the thoughts and intentions of the heart. 13 And no creature is hidden from his sight, but all are naked and exposed to the eyes of him to whom we must give account.

14 Since then we have a great high priest who has passed through the heavens, Jesus, the Son of God, let us hold fast our confession. 15 For we do not have a high priest who is unable to sympathize with our weaknesses, but one who in every respect has been tempted as we are, yet without sin. 16 Let us then with confidence draw near to the throne of grace, that we may receive mercy and find grace to help in time of need.

4. Think about the biblical descriptions of God's Word in verse 12. How does each describe a unique quality of God's Word?

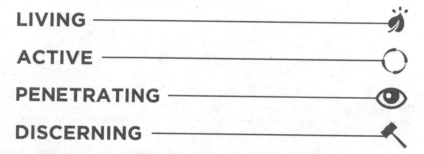

LIVING

ACTIVE

PENETRATING

DISCERNING

"God speaks to us of his purposes and intentions and reveals to us things we cannot learn by looking at the world or listening to our consciences" (*VT*, 43). What makes the Bible different from any other book?

5. Think of a time in your life when the Word of God did its work like a surgeon's scalpel. What Scriptures did God use to penetrate your heart? What was the effect?

6. Why is prayer sometimes a struggle? What does that reveal about our understanding of the gospel and prayer?

7. According to verse 16, how should we approach the "throne of grace"? Why?

TRANSFORM

8. What was something new you learned about prayer or the Bible from chapter three of *Visual Theology*?

9. How would you describe the connection between the Bible and prayer?

10. We began by reflecting on the past two weeks of your relationship with God. What steps can you take to grow closer to Christ through his Word and prayer in the next two weeks? Talk about your plan with your group and how you can encourage one another.

Also, take a close look at the books of the Bible infographic on pages 50–51 of *Visual Theology*. Think creatively about how you might you use this to grow in your own understanding of the Bible or to help others grow.

PERSONAL REFLECTION

1. "A healthy Christian loves to hear from God through the Bible. He is constantly taking in God's Word" (*VT*, 43). Evaluate the different ways you can "take in" God's Word (below and on the next page). Which of these have you experienced recently? Where do you need to grow?

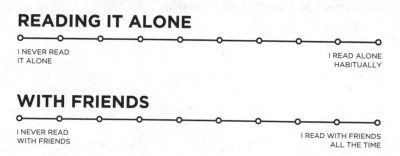

READING IT ALONE

I NEVER READ
IT ALONE

I READ ALONE
HABITUALLY

WITH FRIENDS

I NEVER READ
WITH FRIENDS

I READ WITH FRIENDS
ALL THE TIME

WITH FAMILY

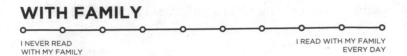

I NEVER READ
WITH MY FAMILY

I READ WITH MY FAMILY
EVERY DAY

READING IT WOVEN INTO GOOD BOOKS

SCRIPTURE IS NOT CONTAINED
IN ANY BOOKS I READ

THIS IS REGULAR
AND NORMAL

HEARING IT READ ALOUD IN WORSHIP SERVICES

NOT READ OUT LOUD
AT ALL

REGULARLY AND SPECIFICALLY
READ OUT LOUD

PONDERING IT

I NEVER THINK
ABOUT SCRIPTURE

I PONDER
CONSTANTLY

2. Prayer is a duty, but it is also a delight. How can something that is a duty also be a delight? Can you think of another "duty" that is also a delight for you? What makes it such a delight?

3. How would you answer the question, "If God is unchangeable, and if he already knows the future, why should I bother praying" (*VT*, 62)?

4. "Christianity offers a genuine relationship with the living God!" (*VT*, 59). Read and think about Colossians 1:9–14.

> [9] And so, from the day we heard, we have not ceased to pray for you, asking that you may be filled with the knowledge of his will in all spiritual wisdom and understanding, [10] so as to walk in a manner worthy of the Lord, fully pleasing to him: bearing fruit in every good work and increasing in the knowledge of God; [11] being strengthened with all power, according to his glorious might, for all endurance and patience with joy; [12] giving thanks to the Father, who has qualified you to share in the inheritance of the saints in light. [13] He has delivered us from the domain of darkness and transferred us to the kingdom of his beloved Son, [14] in whom we have redemption, the forgiveness of sins.

What does Paul pray for?

"Pray as a foretaste of the face-to-face relationships you will enjoy with him forever" (*VT*, 59). Write a prayer in your own words using these verses as a guide.

▣ VISUALIZE

"Our prayers should arise out of immersion in Scripture. We should 'plunge ourselves into the sea' of God's language, the Bible. We should listen, study, think, reflect, and ponder the Scriptures until there is an answering response in our hearts and minds."
—Tim Keller (*VT*, 57)*

"Consider praying in concentric circles from your own soul outward to the whole world. This is my regular practice. I pray for my own soul first. Not because I am more deserving than others, but because if God doesn't awaken and strengthen and humble and fill my own soul, then I can't pray for anybody else's. Then I go to the next concentric circle, my family, and I pray for each of them by name and [then] some of my extended family. Then I go to the next concentric circle, the staff and elders of our church."—John Piper**

On the next page, visualize some truth from this chapter, whether about Scripture, prayer, or the relationship between them, that was a new realization for you or that impacted you afresh.

---

* Tim Keller, *Prayer: Experiencing Awe and Intimacy with God* (New York: Dutton, 2014), 55.
** John Piper, "Devote Yourselves to Prayer." January 9, 2000 http://www.desiringgod.org/messages/devote
-yourselves-to-prayer (accessed June 15, 2016).

CHAPTER FOUR
DRAMA

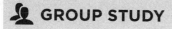 BIG PICTURE

"The Bible tells us we are living within a great story, a great drama. In fact, it tells us this whole universe is a stage that exists to tell a story. You are one of the actors." (*VT*, 65)

- See the unfolding drama of God's plan of redemption in Scripture.
- Learn to interpret the unfolding drama as it is "played out" in our own lives and the lives of those around us.

KEY TERMS TO DEFINE

- **Creation** (*VT*, 67; Genesis 1–2)
- **Fall** (*VT*, 70; Genesis 3)
- **Redemption** (*VT*, 73; Genesis 3:15; 2 Corinthians 5:21; Hebrews 4:15)
- **New Creation** (*VT*, 75; 2 Corinthians 5:17; Revelation 21:4)

GROUP STUDY

 REFLECT

1. Think of a really disappointing story you've seen or read, one where the conclusion wasn't satisfying. What made it so disappointing for you?

2. "If there's a story, there is a storyteller. . . . If there is a story, there is a hero. . . . If there is a story, there is a plot. . . . If there is a story, it is driving toward a conclusion" (*VT*, 66–67). Summarize the four acts of Scripture (see *VT*, 67–75) in your own words.

3. Many people think of Christianity as a religion. How is it helpful to also think about Christianity as a story with a plotline that continues to unfold in history?

4. Everyone needs to wrestle with life's difficult questions (see examples below). Think about how someone who doesn't believe in God would answer these questions. How might other religions answer them? If you're a new Christian, what answers did you give prior to believing the Bible?
   - Who am I?
   - What am I here for?
   - Why is the world so imperfect?
   - Is there any solution to this mess?
   - Is there hope for the future?

"The Bible tells us we are living within a great story, a great drama. In fact, it tells us this whole universe is a stage that exists to tell a story. You are one of the actors" (*VT*, 65). Yet countless people we meet in classrooms and coffee shops live their lives following the wrong script. How does that make us feel? How should we respond? It "greatly distressed" the apostle Paul as he walked through Athens, a city where philosophers and false gods taught that the world was nothing more than matter or ideas and the purpose of life was no greater than avoiding pain or pursuing pleasure. The people of the city were reading the story wrong. And they would continue to miss the drama without the message of the gospel. Patiently and passionately, Paul tried to help them look at their surrounding world through the lens of Scripture to move them away from their own story into the drama of God. Read Acts 17:16–34 below, and then answer the questions that follow.

16 Now while Paul was waiting for them at Athens, his spirit was provoked within him as he saw that the city was full of idols. 17 So he reasoned in the synagogue with the Jews and the devout persons, and in the marketplace every day with those who happened to be there. 18 Some of the Epicurean and Stoic philosophers also conversed with him. And some said, "What does this babbler wish to say?" Others said, "He seems to be a preacher of foreign divinities"—because he was preaching Jesus and the resurrection. 19 And they took him and brought him to the Areopagus, saying, "May we know what this new teaching is that you are presenting? 20 For you bring some strange things to our ears. We wish to know therefore what these things mean." 21 Now all the Athenians and the foreigners who lived there would spend their time in nothing except telling or hearing something new.

22 So Paul, standing in the midst of the Areopagus, said: "Men of Athens, I perceive that in every way you are very religious. 23 For as I passed along and observed the objects of your worship, I found also an altar with this inscription: 'To the unknown god.' What therefore you worship as unknown, this I proclaim to you. 24 The God who made the world and everything in it, being Lord of heaven and earth, does not live in temples made by man, 25 nor is he served by human hands, as though he needed anything, since he himself gives to all mankind life and breath and everything. 26 And he made from one man every nation of mankind to live on all the face of the earth, having determined allotted periods and the boundaries of their dwelling place, 27 that they should seek God, and perhaps feel their way toward him and find him. Yet he is actually not far from each one of us, 28 for

"'In him we live and move and have our being';
as even some of your own poets have said,
"'For we are indeed his offspring.'

[29] Being then God's offspring, we ought not to think that the divine being is like gold or silver or stone, an image formed by the art and imagination of man. [30] The times of ignorance God overlooked, but now he commands all people everywhere to repent, [31] because he has fixed a day on which he will judge the world in righteousness by a man whom he has appointed; and of this he has given assurance to all by raising him from the dead."

[32] Now when they heard of the resurrection of the dead, some mocked. But others said, "We will hear you again about this." [33] So Paul went out from their midst. [34] But some men joined him and believed, among whom also were Dionysius the Areopagite and a woman named Damaris and others with them.

5. Who was Paul's audience? What did they believe?

6. How did Paul introduce his sermon?

7. Using the infographic on the next page, trace the four acts of the unfolding story of the Bible through Paul's message in Acts 17.

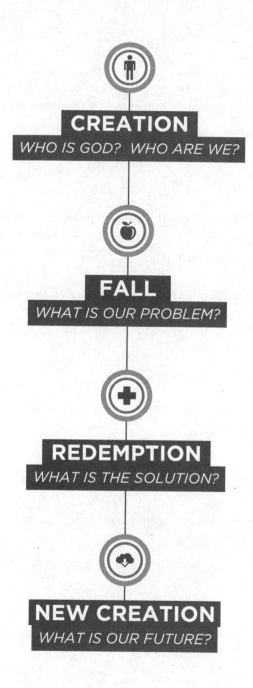

CREATION
WHO IS GOD? WHO ARE WE?

FALL
WHAT IS OUR PROBLEM?

REDEMPTION
WHAT IS THE SOLUTION?

NEW CREATION
WHAT IS OUR FUTURE?

8. If Paul were to visit a classroom or coffee shop, what visual reminders of the gospel might he key in on to help others see the drama of Scripture?

9. Our lives are filled with visual reminders of the drama, but we need to learn to recognize them. Properly recognizing the visual evidences around us will help us remember the unfolding drama.

   What visual reminders of creation surround us? *(Examples: sunsets, the animal world, the power of a storm or the ocean, etc.)*

   What visual reminders of the fall can we find? *(Examples: cemeteries, the seasons of fall and winter, etc.)*

   What visual reminders of redemption are there? *(Examples: church buildings, hospitals, etc.)*

   What visual reminders of the new creation do we see? *(Examples: friendship, the birth of a new child, the season of spring, etc.)*

1. How should the truth that Jesus is the great hero of the story change the way we read, understand, and apply the truth of the Bible?

2. "The greatest joy we experience is just a taste, a hint, of what will be" (*VT*, 75). What joys in your life would you describe as a foretaste of the future?

3. Think of someone in your life who doesn't understand the gospel. How might you talk to them about Jesus in light of what you've learned about the drama of redemption?

4. Read and reflect on Colossians 1:15–20 (below).

    [15] He is the image of the invisible God, the firstborn of all creation. [16] For by him all things were created, in heaven and on earth, visible and invisible, whether thrones or dominions or rulers or authorities—all things were created through him and for him. [17] And he is before all things, and in him all things hold together. [18] And he is the head of the body, the church. He is the beginning, the firstborn from the dead, that in everything he might be preeminent. [19] For in him all the fullness of God was pleased to dwell, [20] and

through him to reconcile to himself all things, whether on earth or in heaven, making peace by the blood of his cross.

How is creation, fall, redemption, and new creation evidenced in this passage?

What does this passage teach us about the purpose of history?

VISUALIZE

Using the space provided on the next page, how would you visualize the four-part drama of Scripture: creation, fall, redemption, and new creation? Or, visualize the great exchange of 2 Corinthians 5:21: "For our sake he made [Jesus] to be sin who knew no sin, so that in him we might become the righteousness of God."

CHAPTER FIVE

DOCTRINE

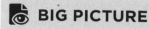 BIG PICTURE

"Doctrine represents the immense privilege God has given you—to know what is really true about him, about yourself and the rest of humanity, and about this world." (*VT*, 79)

- Know and understand the importance of doctrine in the life of every Christian.

KEY TERMS TO DEFINE

- **Doctrine** (*VT*, 79; Acts 2:41–42; Ephesians 4:14; 2 Thessalonians 3:6)

GROUP STUDY

REFLECT

1. What do you think of when you hear the word *doctrine*? Check all the boxes that apply (below and the next page) and explain why.

   ☐ Never heard of it

   ☐ Dry facts

   ☐ Dull and divisive

   ☐ Petty disputes

☐ Exciting and uniting

☐ Rich truths

☐ A privilege

2. What influences (people, events, books), if any, have shaped both your perception and knowledge of doctrine?

 ENCOUNTER

One of the most enduring songs of the church in the last century is "The Church's One Foundation" by Samuel J. Stone. Stone wrote it to help his small parish in Windsor, England, grasp big truths in a language they could understand. So the hymn was simple but rich in Scripture and doctrine. For example, the second stanza is clearly drawing us back to the truths of Ephesians 4:1–16. Speaking of the church, Stone wrote:

> *Elect from every nation,*
> *Yet one o'er all the earth;*
> *Her charter of salvation,*
> *One Lord, one faith, one birth.*
> *One holy Name she blesses,*
> *Partakes one holy food,*
> *And to one hope she presses,*
> *With every grace endued.*

Our lives must be built on knowledge of Christ, and knowledge means doctrine. Jesus is the foundation for our growth, love, worship, humility, obedience, and unity. Christ is the foundation for our growth, and he's also the goal or end of our growth. We long to "become mature, attaining to the whole measure of the fullness of Christ" (Ephesians 4:13).*

3. Read through Ephesians 4:1–16 to see the need for strong doctrine to grow to be like Christ.

> [1] I therefore, a prisoner for the Lord, urge you to walk in a manner worthy of the calling to which you have been called, [2] with all humility and gentleness, with patience, bearing with one another in love, [3] eager to maintain the unity of the Spirit in the bond of peace. [4] There is one body and one Spirit—just as you were called to the one hope that belongs to your call— [5] one Lord, one faith, one baptism, [6] one God and Father of all, who is over all and through all and in all. [7] But grace was given to each one of us according to the measure of Christ's gift. [8] Therefore it says,

> "When he ascended on high he led a host of captives,
>   and he gave gifts to men."

> [9] (In saying, "He ascended," what does it mean but that he had also descended into the lower regions, the earth? [10] He who descended is the one who also ascended far above all the heavens, that he might fill all things.) [11] And he gave the apostles, the prophets, the evangelists, the shepherds and teachers, [12] to equip the saints for the work of ministry, for building up the body of Christ, [13] until we all attain to the unity of the faith and of the knowledge of the Son of God, to mature manhood, to the measure of the stature of the fullness of Christ, [14] so that we may no longer be children, tossed to and fro by the waves and carried about by every wind of doctrine, by human cunning, by craftiness in deceitful schemes. [15] Rather, speaking the truth in love, we are to grow up in every way into him who is the head, into Christ, [16] from whom the whole body, joined and held together by every joint with which it is equipped, when each part is working properly, makes the body grow so that it builds itself up in love.

---

* Tim Challies, "Hymn Stories: The Church's One Foundation." April 28, 2013 http://www.challies.com/articles/hymn-stories-the-churchs-one-foundation-free-download (accessed May 11, 2016).

Now skim through the passage again and use the infographic on the next page, starting at the bottom, to process the content. Then come back and finish the questions below.

What are some threats that we face as we seek to obey Christ?

In verse 11, what gifts does God give his church?

(Verses 7–10 can seem out of place and complicated. They are simply a beautiful poetic way to describe how Christ came down to this earth to provide every Christian every gift we need to follow him.)

What verses describe our humility?

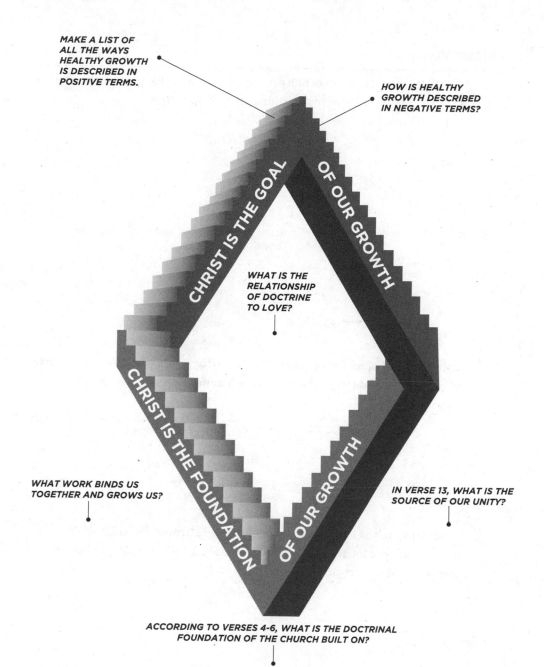

MAKE A LIST OF ALL THE WAYS HEALTHY GROWTH IS DESCRIBED IN POSITIVE TERMS.

HOW IS HEALTHY GROWTH DESCRIBED IN NEGATIVE TERMS?

CHRIST IS THE GOAL OF OUR GROWTH

WHAT IS THE RELATIONSHIP OF DOCTRINE TO LOVE?

CHRIST IS THE FOUNDATION OF OUR GROWTH

WHAT WORK BINDS US TOGETHER AND GROWS US?

IN VERSE 13, WHAT IS THE SOURCE OF OUR UNITY?

ACCORDING TO VERSES 4-6, WHAT IS THE DOCTRINAL FOUNDATION OF THE CHURCH BUILT ON?

4. Why is doctrine the source of unity in the church? What happens when a church attempts to be united around something other than doctrine?

5. Why is it important for every Christian to understand and study doctrine?

6. After reading chapter five of *Visual Theology*, what would you say to a pastor who believed that the best way to keep his church unified was by avoiding doctrinal discussions?

7. What steps can you take in your own life to keep learning doctrine? What doctrines are you interested in learning more about? What theological issues have bothered or intrigued you?

✉ PERSONAL REFLECTION

1. "Part of the joy of singing great hymns of the faith together, and part of the blessing of reciting classic Christian creeds together, is that we do so with a multitude of fellow Christians who are bound together in common faith through a common Savior" (*VT*, 85). How can music serve as a tool for our growth in understanding the work of Christ?

2. Read your church's statement of faith (you'll most likely find it on the church website). What questions, if any, do you have about it?

If you want to dig deeper, study the book of Ephesians and make a list of doctrines mentioned. See how Paul connects them to the Christian life. Try tracing the themes of growth, love, maturity, unity, worship, and humility throughout the book.

3. Read and think about Colossians 2 (below and the next page).

[1] For I want you to know how great a struggle I have for you and for those at Laodicea and for all who have not seen me face to face, [2] that their hearts may be encouraged, being knit together in love, to reach all the riches of full assurance of understanding and the knowledge of God's mystery, which is Christ, [3] in whom are hidden all the treasures of wisdom and knowledge. [4] I say this in order that no one may delude you with plausible arguments. [5] For though I am absent in body, yet I am with you in spirit, rejoicing to see your good order and the firmness of your faith in Christ.

[6] Therefore, as you received Christ Jesus the Lord, so walk in him, [7] rooted and built up in him and established in the faith, just as you were taught, abounding in thanksgiving.

[8] See to it that no one takes you captive by philosophy and empty deceit, according to human tradition, according to the elemental spirits of the world, and not according to Christ. [9] For in him the whole fullness of deity dwells bodily, [10] and you have been filled in him, who is the head of all rule and authority. [11] In him also you were circumcised with a circumcision made without hands, by putting off the body of the flesh, by the circumcision of Christ, [12] having been buried with him in baptism, in which you were also raised with him through faith in the powerful working of God, who raised him from the dead. [13] And you, who were dead in your trespasses and the uncircumcision of your flesh, God made alive together with him, having forgiven us all our trespasses, [14] by canceling the record of debt that stood against us with its legal demands. This he set aside, nailing it to the cross. [15] He disarmed the rulers and authorities and put them to open shame, by triumphing over them in him.

[16] Therefore let no one pass judgment on you in questions of food and drink, or with regard to a festival or a new moon or a Sabbath. [17] These are a shadow of the things to come, but the substance belongs to Christ. [18] Let no one disqualify you, insisting on asceticism and worship of angels, going on in detail about visions, puffed up without reason by his sensuous mind, [19] and not holding fast to the Head, from whom the whole body, nourished and knit together through its joints and ligaments, grows with a growth that is from God.

[20] If with Christ you died to the elemental spirits of the world, why, as if you were still alive in the world, do you submit to regulations— [21] "Do not handle, Do not taste, Do not touch" [22] (referring to things that all perish as they are used)—according to human precepts and teachings? [23] These have indeed an appearance of wisdom in promoting self-made religion and asceticism and severity to the body, but they are of no value in stopping the indulgence of the flesh.

What are some false doctrines we might need to avoid?

What are some of the benefits of studying doctrine?

Visit www.challies.com/topics/quizzes and test your knowledge of Bible doctrines.

4. First Timothy 2:12 and Ephesians 4:7 teach that faithful church leaders teach doctrine. Who is a doctrinal source for you? Consider asking your pastor what resources he recommends for learning doctrine.

▣ VISUALIZE

"Knowledge of biblical doctrine is to the soul as an anchor to the ship, that holds it steady in the midst of the rolling waves of error, or violent winds of persecution."—Thomas Watson (*VT*, 79)*

Ephesians 4:1–16 is rich in doctrinal truth. Read that passage in two or three Bible translations and then, using the space provided on the next page, visualize (in pictures, words, or both) whatever particular idea that God impresses on your heart.

---

* Thomas Watson, *A Body of Divinity: Contained in Sermons upon the Westminster Assembly's Catechism* (1692; reprint, Edinburgh: Banner of Truth, 2012), 4.

CHAPTER SIX
PUTTING OFF

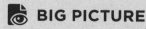 BIG PICTURE

"Very broadly, the Bible lays out two ways you become like Christ: by stopping and by starting. You stop old habits, patterns, and passions, and you start new habits, patterns, and passions." (*VT*, 89)

- We must learn to call out "mistakes" and shortcomings as sin—an offense against God.
- One practical place to begin fighting sin is by "putting off" sins of the mouth.

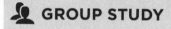 KEY TERMS TO DEFINE

- **Sanctification** (*VT*, 92–93; 1 Corinthians 6:11; 1 Thessalonians 4:3; 5:23)
- **Sin** (*VT*, 94; Romans 3:23)

 GROUP STUDY

REFLECT

1. The word *sin* is not commonly used today. We refer to our "mistakes" or "failures," but we are reluctant to call sin "sin." As a result, we minimize the danger and the effects of sin, but most importantly, we minimize our guilt before God.

   What words do you use to refer to your sin? Why do you use those terms? How do they fall short of calling sin "sin"? (For example, instead of using the word *adultery*, a person might refer to "having an affair." Instead of calling an outburst "anger," someone might say, "I'm just venting.")

2. Think of something you've said recently that you later regretted. Perhaps it was harsh words in a fight, an obscene joke to get a laugh, or a word of gossip to tear someone down. What did you say and why did you say it? What was the result?

 ## ENCOUNTER

We all have different temptations, dispositions, and personalities that make certain sins in our lives more common and challenging for us than for others. One woman's temptation to abuse alcohol may seem foreign to another person who has never been tempted by it. A young man's battle with lust might seem unusual or confusing to another.

Regardless of our individual sins, we all tend to struggle with one area in particular—what we say. Our words are a reflection of our hearts and desires. The book of James calls out the power and abuse of the tongue, describing it as a small spark that "sets on fire the course of our life." The tongue is a "world of evil . . . it corrupts the whole body" (James 3:6).

Controlling our tongue is a first step to developing the discipline of self-control, a fruit of the Holy Spirit's work in our lives. Study the apostle Paul's lists of the sinful things we need to put off in the three passages on the next page, underlining all the commands and circling all the words that relate to sins of speech. Then consider the follow-up question at the top of page 62.

Colossians 3:5–11 (NIV)

5 Put to death, therefore, whatever belongs to your earthly nature: sexual immorality, impurity, lust, evil desires and greed, which is idolatry. 6 Because of these, the wrath of God is coming. 7 You used to walk in these ways, in the life you once lived. 8 But now you must also rid yourselves of all such things as these: anger, rage, malice, slander, and filthy language from your lips. 9 Do not lie to each other, since you have taken off your old self with its practices 10 and have put on the new self, which is being renewed in knowledge in the image of its Creator. 11 Here there is no Gentile or Jew, circumcised or uncircumcised, barbarian, Scythian, slave or free, but Christ is all, and is in all.

Ephesians 4:25–32 (NIV)

25 Therefore each of you must put off falsehood and speak truthfully to your neighbor, for we are all members of one body. 26 "In your anger do not sin": Do not let the sun go down while you are still angry, 27 and do not give the devil a foothold. 28 Anyone who has been stealing must steal no longer, but must work, doing something useful with their own hands, that they may have something to share with those in need.

29 Do not let any unwholesome talk come out of your mouths, but only what is helpful for building others up according to their needs, that it may benefit those who listen. 30 And do not grieve the Holy Spirit of God, with whom you were sealed for the day of redemption. 31 Get rid of all bitterness, rage and anger, brawling and slander, along with every form of malice. 32 Be kind and compassionate to one another, forgiving each other, just as in Christ God forgave you.

Galatians 5:19–21 (NIV)

19 The acts of the flesh are obvious: sexual immorality, impurity and debauchery; 20 idolatry and witchcraft; hatred, discord, jealousy, fits of rage, selfish ambition, dissensions, factions 21 and envy; drunkenness, orgies, and the like. I warn you, as I did before, that those who live like this will not inherit the kingdom of God.

3. How would you categorize these lists of sins in Colossians 3:5–11; Ephesians 4:25–32; and Galatians 5:19–21? What similarities are there between Paul's lists? You might even want to draw lines between the passages to connect reoccurring words.

 TRANSFORM

4. In light of God's Word and what you've learned in chapter six of *Visual Theology*, take a few minutes to individually analyze the situation you shared in question two (or another instance of sinful behavior). Then, as a group, share insights you learn from the process.

   - **Evaluate** – What word would the Bible use to label your sin? Try to be as specific as possible. What does God say about your sin?
   - **Fill** – In what ways were you tempted to minimize your sin? What does your sin do to you, to others, and to God? How would you describe the difference between feeling regret and filling "your mind and conscience with the guilt, the weight, and the evil of your sin" (*VT*, 98)?
   - **Long** – What wrong or incomplete reasons do you have for wanting to sin? What might you desire instead that can free you from your desire for sin?
   - **Consider** – "Consider whether there are ways this sin is amplified by your nature or your natural disposition" (*VT*, 99). Are there aspects of your personality that make this behavior particularly attractive to you? How can you use this knowledge to fight sin rather than excuse it?
   - **Contemplate** – "Think about the times when you tend to fall into this sin. What are the occasions surrounding it? What events happened right before it? What patterns are evident in your sin? What are the habits or patterns that lead to it? What mood or frame of mind tends to precede it?" (*VT*, 100).
   - **Battle** – Tim's first description of battle is helpful. He describes it as humbly crying out to God, rather than having a proud sense of self-sufficiency. When will you most likely be tempted again? What steps can you take now to prepare for the battle or even avoid it in the first place? "Never, ever

allow yourself to toy with sin. Never think you will sin only this far, but no further" (*VT*, 101).

- **Meditate** – What specific truths of Scripture and attributes of God can you meditate on to fuel your sorrow for sin and your longing for holiness? What is your plan to equip yourself for battle?

5. "Think about God. Read his Word and meditate on it. Especially search out the glory of God and think about the massive distance between you and him" (*VT*, 101). Given the chance to replay the situation you described in question two, what would have been different if you had put off sin and put on Christ?

PERSONAL REFLECTION

1. "Stop running back to the grave" (*VT*, 103). Why do you think we feel safer and more at home in our grave clothes? What is it about our sin that makes it so comfortable and familiar?

2. Take a close look at the flowchart on pages 96–97 of *Visual Theology*. Where in the process do you tend to get stuck and deviate toward sin?

3. One of the takeaways from this section is the importance of fully appreciating the gravity of our sin before we confront it with the truth of the gospel. Like the approach to God in the Old Testament, made possible through sacrifices, mediators, and clear laws guiding how the people could draw near to God, we need to appreciate the holiness of the God we serve. What steps do you need to take to truly contemplate the depth of your sin in order to better fight against it?

4. Why is it dangerous to speak peace to yourself before God does?

5. Read and think about Colossians 3:1–11 (verses 1–4 are below; verses 5–11 are on page 61). Pray that God would open your eyes to see the ugliness of sin and the beauty of Christ.

[1] If then you have been raised with Christ, seek the things that are above, where Christ is, seated at the right hand of God. [2] Set your minds on things that are above, not on things that are on earth. [3] For you have died, and your life is hidden with Christ in God. [4] When Christ who is your life appears, then you also will appear with him in glory.

■ VISUALIZE

"Sin is like water held back by a dam." (*VT*, 101)

Think of the most repulsive thing you can imagine . . . because that's what sin is in God's eyes. That also needs to be your mind's picture of *your* own sin. Now, using the space below, visualize sin (in pictures, words, or both), or visualize its effects.

SECTION THREE
BECOME LIKE CHRIST

CHAPTER SEVEN
PUTTING ON

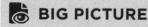 BIG PICTURE

"As a Christian, you cannot merely stop sinning. That is a great thing to do, but not sinning is not enough. You need to pursue the right things. You need to turn away from sin and turn toward righteousness." (*VT*, 107)

- Learn to replace specific vices with specific virtues.
- Understand how to pursue godly character in all virtues.

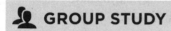 KEY TERMS TO DEFINE

- **Repentance** (*VT*, 110; 2 Corinthians 7; 1 Thessalonians 1:9)
- **Spiritual Disciplines** (*VT*, 113; John 15:7; 16:24; 2 Peter 3:18)

 GROUP STUDY

REFLECT

1. In this section, we refer to putting off our sin and putting on Christ, much like we would do with an article of clothing. As you begin the discussion, share with the group if you have a favorite shirt or other article of clothing. Why do you enjoy wearing this? Is there a story behind it?

2. Share something that makes you really angry. How would people who know you well describe you when you're angry? What helps you calm down?

⬛ ENCOUNTER

What joy there is in knowing that we become like Christ because we are forgiven and not in order to be forgiven! Because of the gospel, there is no sin that cannot be forgiven and no vice that will enslave us forever. "Just as Lazarus walked out of the tomb and began peeling off his grave clothes, we are to walk away from our spiritual deadness and put on spiritual life" (*VT*, 107). To become like Christ, we must battle sin and grow in holiness. We must be honest, humble, and specific in taking off our grave clothes, and equally specific in the virtues we put on. In chapter seven of *Visual Theology*, Tim briefly walked through a portion of Ephesians 4 to show how we replace vice with virtue. In the section that follows, we'll study that Scripture in more detail.

3. Read Ephesians 4:20–24 (below). What does this passage teach us regarding the old self and new self?

> [20] But that is not the way you learned Christ!— [21] assuming that you have heard about him and were taught in him, as the truth is in Jesus, [22] to put off your old self, which belongs to your former manner of life and is corrupt through deceitful desires, [23] and to be renewed in the spirit of your minds, [24] and to put on the new self, created after the likeness of God in true righteousness and holiness.

4. Paul gives five examples of putting off (vices) and putting on (virtues). He then expands each example with a reason for why it should be taken off and what goes in its place. Read the following verses from Ephesians 4 and complete the chart.

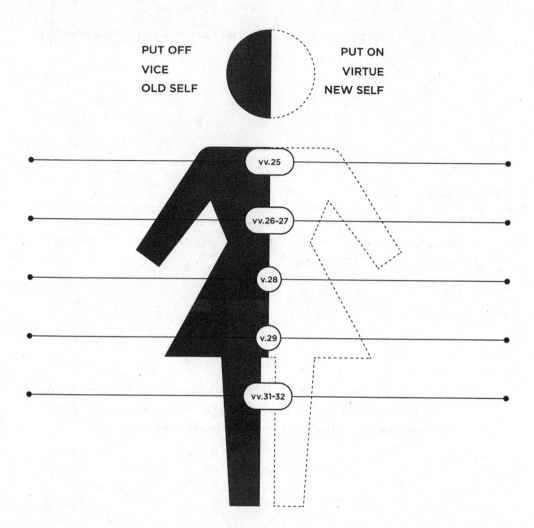

PUT OFF
VICE
OLD SELF

PUT ON
VIRTUE
NEW SELF

vv.25

vv.26-27

v.28

v.29

vv.31-32

5. Vice and virtue are personal and corporate matters. Think about some of the ways the old self tears down the body of Christ. How does the new self build up the body of Christ?

6. How does Paul root this process of putting off and putting on in the gospel? Why does this matter?

▣ TRANSFORM

7. *Before* reading this chapter, how would you have completed the sentence: "True life change demands . . ." or "True life change begins with . . ."? *After* reading this chapter, how would you answer it?

8. "There is not a single virtue in the Bible that I am free to ignore as though it does not pertain to me" (*VT*, 116). What virtues do you tend to downplay or ignore? Are any of these ignored by your community of believers? If so, why?

9. "You will find far more joy and far longer-lasting joy in obedience than you ever did in your disobedience" (*VT*, 117). How have you experienced this to be true in your life? How does this encourage you as you become like Christ?

⊠ PERSONAL REFLECTION

1. Which of the four marks of true repentance that are mentioned in this chapter of *Visual Theology* did you most need to hear about today?

2. Use the infographic on page 114 of *Visual Theology* to consider the fruit of the Spirit in your life. Where have you seen spiritual growth in the past year? If you haven't observed growth, why not?

3. Read and think about Colossians 3:12–17 (below). How does God use his Word and other people to help us become like Christ?

> [12] Put on then, as God's chosen ones, holy and beloved, compassionate hearts, kindness, humility, meekness, and patience, [13] bearing with one another and, if one has a complaint against another, forgiving each other; as the Lord has forgiven you, so you also must forgive. [14] And above all these put on love, which binds everything together in perfect harmony. [15] And let the peace of Christ rule in your hearts, to which indeed you were called in one body. And be thankful. [16] Let the word of Christ dwell in you richly, teaching and admonishing one another in all wisdom, singing psalms and hymns and spiritual songs, with thankfulness in your hearts to God. [17] And whatever you do, in word or deed, do everything in the name of the Lord Jesus, giving thanks to God the Father through him.

▣ VISUALIZE

"If your life is like a glass, that glass is always full. When you take something out, something else rushes in." (*VT*, 115)

Using the space provided on the next page, consider creating an infographic based on Romans 12:1–2 (below) showing how you present your body to God. Or, if another truth from this study of chapter seven has hit home in a new way, visualize that instead.

[1] Therefore, I urge you, brothers and sisters, in view of God's mercy, to offer your bodies as a living sacrifice, holy and pleasing to God—this is your true and proper worship. [2] Do not conform to the pattern of this world, but be transformed by the renewing of your mind. Then you will be able to test and approve what God's will is—his good, pleasing and perfect will. (NIV)

SECTION FOUR
LIVE FOR CHRIST

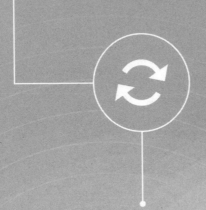

CHAPTER EIGHT
VOCATION

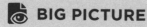 BIG PICTURE

"Our responsibility before God is to understand the gifts, the skills, and the passions he has given us and to use those in fitting ways—in ways that do good to others and, in turn, bring glory to God." (*VT*, 120)

- God is hidden in our vocation, in the various ways we are called to live, and in the relationships we have with others.
- We are all called to extend God's goodness, grace, and order to others.

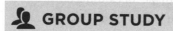 KEY TERMS TO DEFINE

- **Vocation** (*VT*, 120; Genesis 1:28; Matthew 5:16; Ephesians 6:5–9)
- **Sovereignty of God** (*VT*, 126; Isaiah 46:9–11; Romans 11:33–36)

GROUP STUDY

REFLECT

1. In this chapter, we're talking about our work and our jobs. What's the grossest, hardest, or most boring job you've ever had to do?

2. After reading this chapter of *Visual Theology*, what would you describe as your vocations? Which of your various vocations demand the most time? Which of them do you value the most and why?

3. In what way are your vocations a reflection of your values, beliefs, and passions?

![] ENCOUNTER

When a teacher of the law asked Jesus which of the commandments was the most important, Jesus answered, "'Love the Lord your God with all your heart and with all your soul and with all your mind.' This is the first and greatest commandment. And the second is like it: 'Love your neighbor as yourself'" (Matthew 22:37–40 NIV). In other words, God has put us into this world "to bring glory to him by doing good to others" (*VT*, 120). Often, however, the mundaneness of life or the difficulty of work can frustrate us. Have you ever felt like your vocation was getting in the way of really loving God? For example, it can be difficult to see how "God is hidden in vocation" in the middle of changing a diaper or calming down an irate customer. While our vocations can feel like a hindrance at times, even then, they are opportunities to love God and love others.

4. Read as many of the Scripture passages in the infographic on the next page as time permits and study how God, our vocation, and doing good interrelate.

TITUS 2:9–10
COLOSSIANS 3:22–4:1
2 THESSALONIANS 3:6–10
1 TIMOTHY 5:8

1 TIMOTHY 6:17–19
EPHESIANS 4:28
EPHESIANS 6:5–10
1 PETER 2:12

GOD

1. WHAT IS GOD LIKE?

MY VOCATION

2. WHAT PHRASES TELL US HOW WE SHOULD WORK?

3. TO WHOM CAN WE DO GOOD THROUGH OUR WORK?

TRANSFORM

5. What truth about vocation from this chapter of *Visual Theology* encourages you the most?

6. How does your vocation provide you with opportunity to extend God's grace, goodness, and order to others?

PERSONAL REFLECTION

1. In chapter eight of *Visual Theology*, Tim writes that freedom in Christ is not living for yourself. How is this different from how many people define freedom? What is true freedom, according to the Bible?

2. How does the doctrine of vocation lead to love, humility, obedience, healthy growth, and unity?

3. Use the infographic on page 123 of *Visual Theology* to think about and describe your own being, passions, and calling.

4. Read and think about Colossians 3:22–4:1 (below), and then answer the questions that follow.

[22] Bondservants, obey in everything those who are your earthly masters, not by way of eye-service, as people-pleasers, but with sincerity of heart, fearing the Lord. [23] Whatever you do, work heartily, as for the Lord and not for men, [24] knowing that from the Lord you will receive the inheritance as your reward. You are serving the Lord Christ. [25] For the wrongdoer will be paid back for the wrong he has done, and there is no partiality.

[4:1] Masters, treat your bondservants justly and fairly, knowing that you also have a Master in heaven.

Who are you serving?

What knowledge motivates your work?

How should you work?

5. Offer a prayer specifically for your employer and/or employees. Write it here if you would like.

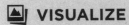 **VISUALIZE**

"Vocation leads to worship." (*VT*, 126)

How does the mandate to work spread God's glory? How does Jesus ultimately complete this? Turn these ideas (or anything else from this chapter of *Visual Theology* that really spoke to you) into pictures, words, or both. Use the space provided on the next page.

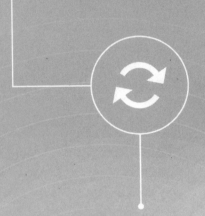

CHAPTER NINE
RELATIONSHIPS

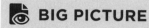 BIG PICTURE

"For the sake of order, and in order to reflect his authority, [God] created patterns of leading and following, roles that would involve exercising authority and roles that would involve submitting to authority. Each one of us takes on both of those roles at different times and in different contexts." (*VT*, 129)

- To grow in godliness, we must learn to imitate the example of Christ.
- Understand the practice and the ministry of reconciliation in your relationships with others.

KEY TERMS TO DEFINE

- **Reconciliation** (*VT*, 129; 2 Corinthians 5:18–21; Colossians 1:19–20)

GROUP STUDY

REFLECT

1. Think about some of the close friendships you have had over the years. Describe one or two of your closest friends. What led you to become friends? What has sustained the friendship over time?

2. "While some of us are called to lead some of the time, all of us are called to submit all of the time" (*VT*, 130). Which of your relationships call you to joyful submission? Which to servant leadership?

3. Think of a time when you had to do something you didn't want to do. To whose authority were you responding, and what was the task? What was it about the task that made you not want to do it?

🔔 ENCOUNTER

"We imitate Christ in his loving leadership. We imitate Christ in his servant-hearted submission. We imitate Christ in his deep, spiritual friendships. We live for him, through him, and in imitation of him" (*VT*, 139). If we are to imitate Christ in his relationships, we must learn from his relationships. Jesus the Son of God has always existed in perfect relationship with the Father. In his humanity, Jesus is the perfect son, perfect sibling, perfect friend, and perfect leader. Although he commands the armies of heaven, he submitted to the Roman Empire. Although one day every knee will bow before him, Jesus joyfully submitted to his earthly parents, Mary and Joseph. Jesus had close friendships full of laughter and tears, and even friends that deserted him. It is likely that Jesus also had relationships with coworkers or customers.

All of Jesus's relationships are instructive for us. In this chapter, we will study various passages to learn about the relationships of Jesus during his earthly ministry.

4. Read as many of the following Scriptures as time permits. What words or phrases show us Christ's motivation in his relationships with others? Use the chart to jot your responses.

Matthew 22:15–22	
John 8:27–30	
Luke 2:41–52	
Matthew 5:38–48	
Matthew 20:25–28	
John 13:1–17	
John 15:12–15	

5. What does your study of Jesus's motivation say about our motivation for pursuing relationships? What can we learn to imitate from the relationships of Jesus?

 TRANSFORM

6. Take a minute or two to review the "one another" infographic on pages 136–137 of *Visual Theology*. In which areas would you say your Christian community typically does well? In which areas does it need improvement? (That community, of course, includes you!)

7. Look back to question three and describe how you could have imitated Christ in that situation. Where could you have found joy in the midst of anger, annoyance, or aggravation?

8. Share some practical ways you can serve those you lead or show joy in relationships that call you to submit.

PERSONAL REFLECTION

1. Consider once more the infographic on pages 136–137 of *Visual Theology*. How have other Christians assisted your growth in becoming more like Christ? What relationships are you building into right now, for the good of the other person?

2. What is one way this week you can encourage someone you lead or someone you follow?

3. Read and think about Colossians 3:18–4:1 (verses 18–21 are below; see page 79 for the remainder of the passage). What is the reason given for each command?

> [18] Wives, submit to your husbands, as is fitting in the Lord. [19] Husbands, love your wives, and do not be harsh with them. [20] Children, obey your parents in everything, for this pleases the Lord. [21] Fathers, do not provoke your children, lest they become discouraged.

4. Pray through the different spheres of your relationships, asking God specifically to empower your servant leadership and joyful submission. If you'd like, record a written prayer here.

◩ VISUALIZE

"What God accomplished through the death and resurrection of Christ was a great act of reconciliation." (*VT*, 129)

As the apostle Paul writes in 2 Corinthians 5:18–19:

> [18] All this [the fact of our new creation] is from God, who through Christ reconciled us to himself and gave us the ministry of reconciliation; [19] that is, in Christ God was reconciling the world to himself, not counting their trespasses against them, and entrusting to us the message of reconciliation.

Using pictures, words, or both, visualize this amazing news—and what it means to you personally. Space is provided on the next page.

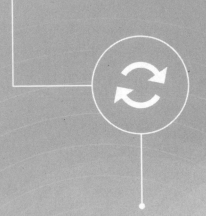

SECTION FOUR
LIVE FOR CHRIST

CHAPTER TEN

STEWARDSHIP

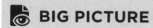

BIG PICTURE

"The principle of stewardship is built on two simple premises: God owns it, and you manage it." (*VT*, 141)

- Learn about the principle of stewardship.
- Begin investing in eternity and focusing each day on the gospel.

KEY TERMS TO DEFINE

- **Stewardship** (*VT*, 141; Mark 4:21–25; 1 Corinthians 4:2; Ephesians 5:15–17)

GROUP STUDY

 ### REFLECT

1. When you need to purchase something, do you prefer to shop online or go to an actual retail outlet? Why?

2. Whether it's coffee, clothing, candy, or even cars, many people are prone to impulse buying. A good test of our financial stewardship is what we buy on an impulse. What are you tempted to buy on an impulse?

3. What immediate satisfaction do you get from impulse purchases? Talk about how you justify it to yourself or your spouse or perhaps your parents (if you're living at home). What might your answers reveal about your understanding of what it means to be a steward?

🗨 ENCOUNTER

"Moreover, it is required of stewards that they be found faithful" (1 Corinthians 4:2). We are called to faithfully steward the gospel, our time and money, and even our bodies. As we seek to be faithful stewards we can face two opposing temptations. We can live as if the only things that matter are things we own on earth, or we can live as if nothing on this earth matters. Both ways fail to understand the principle of stewardship.

On the one hand, we are all in daily danger of being swept along in this world, blinded to what is eternally important by promises of power and pleasure and possessions. Sadly, many people have their faith choked out by the cares of this world. But God has also blessed this world with many wonderful gifts for our enjoyment. To reject them is to reject the goodness of God.

4. Read 1 Timothy 6:6–19 (below) to see what you can learn about stewardship from what Paul taught Timothy. Then answer the questions in the chart that follows.

[6] But godliness with contentment is great gain, [7] for we brought nothing into the world, and we cannot take anything out of the world. [8] But if we have food and clothing, with these we will be content. [9] But those who desire to be rich fall into temptation, into a snare, into many senseless and harmful desires that plunge people into ruin and destruction. [10] For the love of money is a root of all kinds of evils. It is through this craving that some have wandered away from the faith and pierced themselves with many pangs.

[11] But as for you, O man of God, flee these things. Pursue righteousness, godliness, faith, love, steadfastness, gentleness. [12] Fight the good fight of the

faith. Take hold of the eternal life to which you were called and about which you made the good confession in the presence of many witnesses. [13] I charge you in the presence of God, who gives life to all things, and of Christ Jesus, who in his testimony before Pontius Pilate made the good confession, [14] to keep the commandment unstained and free from reproach until the appearing of our Lord Jesus Christ, [15] which he will display at the proper time—he who is the blessed and only Sovereign, the King of kings and Lord of lords, [16] who alone has immortality, who dwells in unapproachable light, whom no one has ever seen or can see. To him be honor and eternal dominion. Amen.

[17] As for the rich in this present age, charge them not to be haughty, nor to set their hopes on the uncertainty of riches, but on God, who richly provides us with everything to enjoy. [18] They are to do good, to be rich in good works, to be generous and ready to share, [19] thus storing up treasure for themselves as a good foundation for the future, so that they may take hold of that which is truly life.

Focus on the Gospel	Seek Wisdom	Invest in Eternity
Where are we tempted to find our worth? What is our greatest possession?	Is wealth bad? What temptations come with wealth?	What attributes of God does Paul use to encourage Timothy?
What truths about the gospel does Paul use to encourage Timothy?	What virtues should we seek instead of wealth?	How can we invest in eternity?

5. Upon what two premises is the principle of stewardship built? How would you explain to a friend what it means to be a steward?

6. When we release our ownership over money, we are freed to be generous with it. One of the ways God asks us to prove our stewardship over money is by giving it away. How does generosity prove faithful stewardship?

7. What is stewardship calling you to do regarding your impulse buys? Apply the three principles from the infographic on page 149 of *Visual Theology*.

PERSONAL REFLECTION

1. In which possessions or abilities are you tempted to find your worth instead of the gospel?

2. What does holding onto our resources prove about our beliefs?

3. If you could add another section to the infographic on page 149 of *Visual Theology*, what would it be and what would it say?

4. With whom are you currently seeking to share the gospel?

5. Read and think about Colossians 4:5–18 (below), and then answer the questions that follow.

[5] Walk in wisdom toward outsiders, making the best use of the time. [6] Let your speech always be gracious, seasoned with salt, so that you may know how you ought to answer each person.

[7] Tychicus will tell you all about my activities. He is a beloved brother and faithful minister and fellow servant in the Lord. [8] I have sent him to you for this very purpose, that you may know how we are and that he may encourage your hearts, [9] and with him Onesimus, our faithful and beloved brother, who is one of you. They will tell you of everything that has taken place here.

[10] Aristarchus my fellow prisoner greets you, and Mark the cousin of Barnabas (concerning whom you have received instructions—if he comes to you, welcome him), [11] and Jesus who is called Justus. These are the only men

of the circumcision among my fellow workers for the kingdom of God, and they have been a comfort to me. [12] Epaphras, who is one of you, a servant of Christ Jesus, greets you, always struggling on your behalf in his prayers, that you may stand mature and fully assured in all the will of God. [13] For I bear him witness that he has worked hard for you and for those in Laodicea and in Hierapolis. [14] Luke the beloved physician greets you, as does Demas. [15] Give my greetings to the brothers at Laodicea, and to Nympha and the church in her house. [16] And when this letter has been read among you, have it also read in the church of the Laodiceans; and see that you also read the letter from Laodicea. [17] And say to Archippus, "See that you fulfill the ministry that you have received in the Lord."

[18] I, Paul, write this greeting with my own hand. Remember my chains. Grace be with you.

What does this passage say about our time?

How does Paul encourage the Colossians to steward treasures?

6. Spend a moment praising God for the faithful stewards who shared the gospel with you. Write your prayer of praise here, if you'd like.

▣ VISUALIZE

"You can't take it with you—but you *can* send it on ahead."—Randy Alcorn (*VT*, 145)*

Deuteronomy 10:14 captures our reality succinctly: "Behold, to the Lord your God belong heaven and the heaven of heavens, the earth with all that is in it." Visualize this truth in pictures, words, or both as well as your response.

---

* Randy Alcorn, *The Treasure Principle: Unlocking the Secret of Joyful Giving* (Colorado Springs: Multnomah, 2001), 18.

VISUAL THEOLOGY SERIES GUIDE

FOUR-WEEK OPTION

OVERVIEW

This Series Guide provides an outline of how you can utilize *Visual Theology* as a four-week lesson series or sermon series on the Christian life. Here are some practical suggestions on how you might integrate *Visual Theology* into your ministry: (1) teach *Visual Theology* as a class for new believers to introduce them to the Christian life; (2) preach a miniseries helping your audience assess their spiritual health; (3) coordinate *Visual Theology* with themes from the book of Colossians.

The following guidelines will help you prepare for your series:

1. Before your series, begin by reading through all of *Visual Theology*. The whole book. This will help you become familiar with the material.

2. Pray for your series. Pray that God would first work in your own heart by using his Word to grow you closer to Christ. Pray for the individuals who are in your audience. With the apostle Paul, pray that your group may have the eyes of their heart enlightened in order to know how glorious Christ is (Ephesians 1:18).

3. Prepare for each lesson by reading the corresponding chapters in the book and the related Scripture passages. *Visual Theology* should help you with your study of Scripture, not replace your study. The best teachers own their material. Even if the outlines and illustrations are not your own, make it your own through study and meditation.

4. Consider working through the study guide on your own, both the group and personal reflection questions. Doing so in advance will encourage you as well as provide you with attention-grabbers, illustrations, and applications.

5. Think about the best way to communicate to your audience. You are best positioned to know the specific needs of your group or class. What illustrations will capture their attention? What applications will most speak to your context?

6. Provide follow-up questions to your audience for discussion and personal application. Care for your group by investing in them personally. Continue to pray for them and encourage them.

OVERVIEW

Theme: Grow close to Christ (*VT*, chapters 1–3)
Scripture Passages: Psalm 19:7–11; Matthew 6:5–13; Romans 8:1; 1 Corinthians 15:1–8
Key Concept: "Our first and most basic discipline is cultivating and growing into that personal relationship with Jesus as we hear from him, speak to him, and worship him" (*VT*, 7).

OUTLINE

I.   Gospel – Never move beyond the gospel

II. Identity – Know who you are in Christ

III. Relationship – Grow close through the Bible and prayer

LESSON

Key Concept: "One thing that distinguishes Christianity from every other faith in the world is that Christianity is not only a religion but also a relationship. Some have repeated this so often that it can begin to sound trite or cliché, but let's not lose the wonder of this marvelous fact: Christianity is a religion based on a relationship with a person. As Christians, we have entered into a real and living relationship with the Creator of the universe. And as Christians, our first and most basic discipline is cultivating and growing into that personal relationship with Jesus as we hear from him, speak to him, and worship him" (*VT*, 13).

I.   Gospel – Never move beyond the gospel

   A. Pursue Christ through the gospel

      "The gospel is objective and universal fact that is true for all people through all time. . . . But the gospel is also something every Christian experiences in a unique and personal way. In this sense, gospel is both an announcement and an experience" (*VT*, 19).

B. Recount the gospel

What is the gospel? "God sent his Son Jesus into the world in the power of the Spirit in order to live a perfect life, die a substitutionary death, and rise victorious from the grave (1 Corinthians 15:1–8). This gospel (or good news) is offered to everyone so that all who believe this message are saved from their sins (Romans 10:9–13)" (*VT*, 19).

"Many Christians live with the sad delusion that the gospel is only the entrance-way to the Christian life. They believe that the gospel gets you in, but then you need to advance to deeds, creeds, and meeting needs. But the good news never becomes old news" (*VT*, 21).

II. Identity – Know who you are in Christ

"As you attempt to live a spiritually healthy life and as you grow close to Christ, it is absolutely crucial that you understand who you have become and who you are" (*VT*, 29).

A. I am in Christ (1 Corinthians 15:22).

B. I am justified (Romans 8:1).

C. I am adopted (John 1:12).

D. I am secure (Romans 8:38–39).

E. I am free (Romans 6:5–6).

F. I am unfinished (Philippians 1:6).

III. Relationship – Grow close through the Bible and prayer

"A healthy Christian loves to hear from God through the Bible. He is constantly taking in God's Word—reading it alone, reading it with friends, reading it with family, reading it as it is woven into good books, hearing it aloud in worship services, pondering it as he remembers it—consuming it in any way he can" (*VT*, 43).

A. Through the Bible (Psalm 19:7–11)

B. Through prayer (Matthew 6:5–13)

FOLLOW-UP QUESTIONS

- What are some practical ways you can share the story of your conversion with someone?
- Which of the identities in Christ that you learned about are the most meaningful to you right now?
- What steps can you take to grow close to Christ through his Word and prayer in the next two weeks?

WEEK 2

OVERVIEW

Theme: Understand the work of Christ (*VT*, chapters 4–5)
Scripture Passages: Genesis 1–3, Ephesians 4:1–16; Colossians 2
Key Concept: "We need to grow in our understanding of what God is accomplishing in this world through the work of Christ. As we do that, we will also grow in our knowledge of God himself so we can better understand who he is and what he is like" (*VT*, 13).

OUTLINE

I.   Drama – We need to understand what God is doing in this world

II. Doctrine – We need to understand who God is in order to grow

LESSON

Key Concept: "The Christian faith involves a relationship, but a relationship requires knowing things about the person as well, especially who they are and what they love to do. So there is also an essential content dimension to the Christian faith—information we need to know and facts we need to understand. Our emphasis in this second discipline is primarily on understanding the work of Christ. We need to grow in our understanding of what God is accomplishing in this world through the work of Christ. As we do that, we will also grow in our knowledge of God himself so we can better understand who he is and what he is like" (*VT*, 13).

I.   Drama – We need to understand what God is doing in this world

"The Bible tells us we are living within a great story, a great drama. In fact, it tells us this whole universe is a stage that exists to tell a story. You are one of the actors" (*VT*, 65).

A. Act 1: Creation (Genesis 1:1, 26, 31; Psalm 100:3)

B. Act 2: Fall (Genesis 3:6, 23; Isaiah 59:2; 24:6)

C. Act 3: Redemption (1 Corinthians 15:3–4; 2 Corinthians 5:21; Ephesians 1:7; Hebrews 4:15)

D. Act 4: New Creation (Psalm 103:12; Luke 1:32–33; 2 Corinthians 5:17; Revelation 21:4)

II. Doctrine – We need to understand who God is in order to grow

"Doctrine represents the immense privilege God has given you—to know what is really true about him, about yourself and the rest of humanity, and about this world" (*VT*, 79).

A. Doctrine leads to love.

B. Doctrine leads to humility.

C. Doctrine leads to obedience.

D. Doctrine leads to unity.

E. Doctrine leads to worship.

F. Doctrine leads to healthy growth.

FOLLOW-UP QUESTIONS

- How should the truth that Jesus is the great hero of the story change the way we read, understand, and apply the truth of the Bible?
- What steps can you take in your own life to keep learning doctrine? What doctrines are you interested in learning more about?
- Who is a doctrinal source for you? Consider asking your pastor what resources he recommends to learn doctrine.

OVERVIEW

Theme: Become like Christ (*VT*, chapters 6–7)

Scripture Passages: Romans 13:11–14; Galatians 5:22–23; Ephesians 4:20–32; Colossians 3:5–14

Key Concept: "The Bible tells us that our purpose in life is to be conformed to his image—to think like him, to speak like him, to behave like him. We do this by putting away old habits, patterns, and passions and by replacing them with new and better habits, patterns, and passions" (*VT*, 14).

OUTLINE

I.   Putting Off – God calls you to kill old habits, patterns, and passions

II. Putting On – God calls you to grow in specific obedience and general obedience

LESSON

Key Concept: "As we grow close to Christ and as we grow in our knowledge of his work, we will find ourselves with a longing to become like him. The Bible tells us that our purpose in life is to be conformed to his image—to think like him, to speak like him, to behave like him. We do this by putting away old habits, patterns, and passions and by replacing them with new and better habits, patterns, and passions" (*VT*, 14).

I.   Putting Off – God calls you to kill old habits, patterns, and passions.

This series of steps is adapted from John Owen's book *Overcoming Sin and Temptation*.

A. Evaluate

B. Fill

C. Consider

D. Long

E. Contemplate

F. Meditate

G. Battle

H. Expect

II. Putting On – God calls you to grow in specific obedience and general obedience

    A. Replace – We must specifically replace vice with virtue

    B. Pursue – We must generally pursue godly character

FOLLOW-UP QUESTIONS

- In what ways are you tempted to minimize your sin or make excuses?
- What truths of Scripture and attributes of God can you meditate on to fuel your sorrow for sin and your longing for holiness?
- What specific virtues is God calling you to put on through the power of the gospel?

OVERVIEW

Theme: Live for Christ (*VT*, chapters 8–10)
Scripture Passages: Romans 12:1–13:2; Ephesians 5:15–6:3; Colossians 3:18–4:5
Key Concept: "We need to learn to live as Christians, to love as Christians, and to serve as Christians—to do all we do in a distinctly Christian way" (*VT*, 14).

OUTLINE

I.   Vocation – We extend God's order, goodness, and grace to others in our vocation

II. Relationships – We serve as ambassadors of reconciliation in our relationships

III. Stewardship – We bring glory to God and enjoy his gifts through our stewardship

LESSON

Key Concept: "We need to learn to live for Christ from the moment we wake up each day to the moment we fall asleep, to live in such a way that we draw attention to him and bring glory to him. We need to learn to live as Christians, to love as Christians, and to serve as Christians—to do all we do in a distinctly Christian way" (*VT*, 14). We live out the gospel in our vocation, relationships, and stewardship.

I.   Vocation – We extend God's order, goodness, and grace to others in our vocation

"What we do is closely related to who we are. And as a Christian, you are responsible to give all of who you are and what you do to the Lord" (*VT*, 119).

A. You have many vocations.

B. Vocation brings dignity.

C. Vocation leads to worship.

II. Relationships – We serve as ambassadors of reconciliation in our relationships

"We live in constant relationship with others. We are born into an existing relationship with parents and siblings and soon develop many more. Some of these are peer relationships, but the ones that the Bible takes special care to address are those in which each person plays a different role and especially in which God means for there to be a pattern of leadership and submission" (*VT*, 129).

III. Stewardship – We bring glory to God and enjoy his gifts through our stewardship

"The principle of stewardship is built on two simple premises: God owns it, and you manage it" (*VT*, 141).

A. Focus on the gospel.

B. Seek wisdom.

C. Invest in eternity.

FOLLOW-UP QUESTIONS

- How does your vocation provide you with opportunity to extend God's grace, goodness, and order to others?
- In what possessions or abilities are you tempted to find your worth, other than the gospel?
- What is one way this week you can encourage someone you lead or someone you follow?

Visual Theology

Seeing and Understanding the Truth About God

Tim Challies and Josh Byers

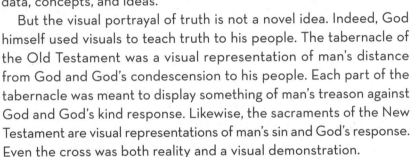

We live in a visual culture. Today, people increasingly rely upon visuals to help them understand new and difficult concepts. The rise and stunning popularity of the internet infographic has given us a new way in which to convey data, concepts, and ideas.

But the visual portrayal of truth is not a novel idea. Indeed, God himself used visuals to teach truth to his people. The tabernacle of the Old Testament was a visual representation of man's distance from God and God's condescension to his people. Each part of the tabernacle was meant to display something of man's treason against God and God's kind response. Likewise, the sacraments of the New Testament are visual representations of man's sin and God's response. Even the cross was both reality and a visual demonstration.

As teachers and lovers of sound theology, Challies and Byers have a deep desire to convey the concepts and principles of systematic theology in a fresh, beautiful, and informative way. In this book, they have made the deepest truths of the Bible accessible in a way that can be seen and understood by a visual generation.

Available in stores and online!

ZONDERVAN®
.com

FIND MORE RESOURCES ONLINE
VISUALTHEOLOGY.CHURCH

PRESENTATION SLIDES
POWERPOINT • KEYNOTE • PROPRESENTER & MORE
OVER 190 SLIDES • EVERY GRAPHIC IN BOOK • BUILDS FOR EACH GRAPHIC • BACKGROUNDS & BLANK SLIDES

POSTERS & GRAPHIC DOWNLOADS
GET POSTER SIZED PRINTS OF EVERY GRAPHIC FROM THE BOOK, OR DOWNLOAD AND PRINT ON YOUR OWN.

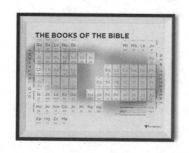
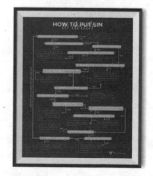